ANSEL ADAMS

1995 Engagement Calendar

Little, Brown and Company

Boston • New York • Toronto • London

Cover: Pine Forest in Snow, Yosemite National Park, California, 1933

New Moon

First Quarter

Full Moon

Last Quarter

ISBN 0—8212—2090—X

Published simultaneously in Canada by Little, Brown & Company (Canada) Limited

Designed by John Kane
Imagesetting in Monotype Bembo by Graphics Express
Printed by Gardner Lithograph

PRINTED IN THE UNITED STATES OF AMERICA

ANSEL ADAMS

A good photographer is like a good cook. Cooking is judged chiefly by the way the food tastes, not by the way it is prepared. After all, a photograph is something to look at; it is supposed to convey something to the mind, to the heart, or to both at the same time. If it is a good photograph it will convey its message; if it is a bad photograph it will not. A bad photograph can convey a bald fact; a good photograph will give the fact another dimension—conviction. A supremely good photograph will give the fact still another dimension—universality.

From "An Approach to a Practical Technique," an article for *U.S. Camera*, 1940

El Capitan, Winter, Sunrise, Yosemite National Park, California, 1968

Evening Cloud, Ellery Lake, Sierra Nevada, California, 1934

Pine Forest in Snow, Yosemite National Park, California, 1933

Clearing Winter Storm, Yosemite National Park, California, 1944

Lone Pine Peak, Sierra Nevada, California, c. 1960

From the Ahwahnee Hotel, Winter, Yosemite National Park, California, 1927

Evening Clouds and Pool, East Side of the Sierra Nevada from the Owens Valley, California, c. 1962

Wood Carving by George Lopez, Cordova, New Mexico, c. 1960

The White Church, Hornitos, California, 1946

Alfred Stieglitz and Painting by Georgia O'Keeffe, at An American Place, New York City, 1944

Grass, Reeds, Water, near Little River, Northern California, 1959

Stream, Sea, Clouds, Rodeo Lagoon, Northern California, 1962

Waterfall, Zion National Park, Utah, 1947

Wrecked Hull, Drakes Bay, Point Reyes National Seashore, California, 1953

In Cedar Breaks National Monument, Utah, c. 1947

North House, Taos Pueblo, New Mexico, 1929

New Church, Taos Pueblo, New Mexico, 1929

Manly Beacon, Death Valley National Monument, California, c. 1948

Rose and Driftwood, San Francisco, California, 1932

Conservatory, Golden Gate Park, San Francisco, California, 1962

Trailside, near Juneau, Alaska, 1947

Grass in Rain, Glacier Bay National Monument, Alaska, 1948

Upper Yosemite Falls, Yosemite National Park, California, c. 1935

Yosemite Falls, Azaleas, Yosemite National Park, California, c. 1940

Lower Yosemite Falls, Yosemite National Park, California, c. 1946

Pool and Cloud Reflections, Glacier Point Road, Yosemite National Park, California, c. 1945

Firehole River, Yellowstone National Park, Wyoming, 1942

Fern Spring, Dusk, Yosemite National Park, California, c. 1961

Siesta Lake, Yosemite National Park, California, c. 1958

Mount Brewer and Bullfrog Lake, Kings Canyon National Park, California, c. 1925

Redwood Grove, Northern California, 1964

Mount Kaweah, Moraine Lake, Sequoia National Park, California, c. 1932

Cliff Palace Ruin, Mesa Verde National Park, Colorado, 1941

Sand Dunes, Death Valley National Monument, California, 1952

Surf and Sky, Hanakapiai, Kauai, Hawaii, c. 1956

The Grand Canyon from Point Sublime, Grand Canyon National Park, Arizona, 1942

From Hurricane Hill, Olympic National Park, Washington, c. 1950

Forest, Autumn, Yosemite National Park, California, 1965

Poplars, Autumn, Owens Valley, California, c. 1937

Road and Fog, Del Monte Forest, Pebble Beach, California, 1964

White House Ruin, Canyon de Chelly National Monument, Arizona, 1942

Thunderstorm over the Great Plains, near Cimarron, New Mexico, 1961

Buttress of West Tower, Mission San Xavier del Bac, Tucson, Arizona, c. 1958

Aspens, Northern New Mexico, 1958

Santuario de Chimayo, New Mexico, c. 1950

Coast South of Cape Sebastian, Oregon, 1968

Grass on Water, Sierra Nevada, California, c. 1935

Coast Looking Southward to Point Reyes National Seashore, California, 1958

Lone Pike Peak and Alabama Hills, California, 1949

Oak Tree in Snow, Yosemite National Park, California, c. 1933

Grounded Iceberg, Glacier Bay National Monument, Alaska, 1948

The Sentinel through Trees, Winter, Yosemite National Park, California, 1960

Half Dome, Blowing Snow, Yosemite National Park, California, c. 1955